IMAGES
of America

WILLOWBROOK
BALLROOM

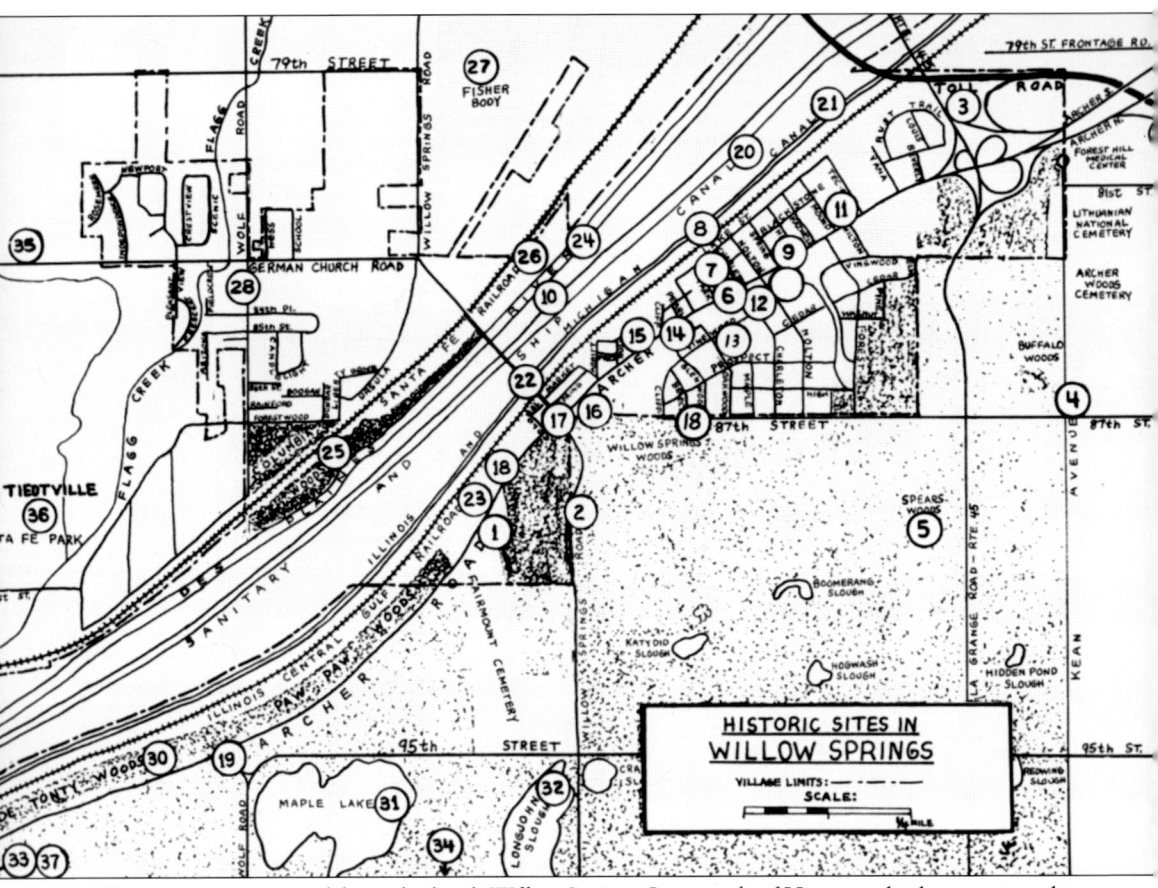

This is a map extracted from the book *Willow Springs Crossroads of History*, which was printed in the 1970s by the Willow Springs Chamber of Commerce. Identified by numbers are the following historical sites: 1. Archer Road (now Archer Avenue); 2. Willow Springs Road; 3. Molenar Farm; 4. Kean Avenue; 5. Spears Woods; 6. downtown Mt. Forest; 7. First Village Hall; 8. Mt. Forest Depot; 9. the second oldest public school, the oldest church, and Mt. Forest Evangelical Congregational Church; 10. Lake Willow Springs; 11. Indian Burial Mounds; 12. Dietrich Mansion; 13. The first public school; 14. Mary Rotz Hletko Wildlife Sanctuary; 15. home of Dr. John W. Rust Sr.; 16. first white settler; 17. first school, ancient Indian Burial Mound, and Indian Trails Trading Post; 18. Willowbrook Ballroom; 19. Ninety-fifth Street and Archer Road; 20. Sanitary and Ship Canal; 21. Illinois and Michigan Canal; 22. origin of Willow Springs' name; 23. Chicago and Alton Railroads; 24. Des Plaines River; 25. Joliet and Marquette; 26. Santa Fe Railroad; 27. Indian Burial Mound; 28. the Land of the Healing Waters and the Council of the Seven Waters; 29. Rosary Hill Convalescent Home; 30. Detonti Woods; 31. Maple Lake; 32. Long John Slough and Wentworth Avenue; 33. St. James Church; 34. Little Red Schoolhouse; 35. Trinity Lutheran Church; 36. Tiedtville; 37. Manhattan Project. (Courtesy of Cindy Carr.)

ON THE COVER: This image of the renowned Lawrence Welk Orchestra was taken at the Willowbrook Ballroom in 1971. (Courtesy of Mike Stosich.)

IMAGES
of America

WILLOWBROOK
BALLROOM

Bonnie Classen

ARCADIA
PUBLISHING

Published by Arcadia Publishing
Charleston, South Carolina

Printed in the United States of America

Library of Congress Control Number: 2011927751

For all general information, please contact Arcadia Publishing:
Telephone 843-853-2070
Fax 843-853-0044
E-mail sales@arcadiapublishing.com
For customer service and orders:
Toll-Free 1-888-313-2665

Visit us on the Internet at www.arcadiapublishing.com

This book is dedicated to all those who understand and appreciate the beauty and necessity of self-expression through the art of music and dancing at the legendary Willowbrook Ballroom

CONTENTS

ACKNOWLEDGMENTS

A special thanks to Pat Williams Verderbar, granddaughter of John and Margaret Verderbar, the original owners of the Oh Henry–turned–Willowbrook Ballroom. Despite a hectic schedule, Pat searched through endless boxes of vintage family photographs and memorabilia that made this book possible. Thank you for sharing the history of three generations of Verderbars whose hard work, dedication, and determination collectively brought joy to millions of patrons through the song and dance of life at this legendary venue. Without the Verderbars, there would be no Willowbrook Ballroom.

Great appreciation is also extended to the current Willowbrook owners, Gedaminis and Birute Jodwalis, for their contribution in sharing the dozens of priceless photographs featuring famous rock bands and big band orchestras from the past, present, and future. Thank you also for the assistance of Rasa Miliauskas, and for keeping the magic alive.

My heart overflows with gratitude toward Mike Stosich, my jackpot contributor of over 60 spectacular photographs featuring grand entertainers from the 1960s and 1970s.

Thank you also to Teddy Lee Jr., son of the late Teddy Lee Sr., for your contribution. This highly favored, talented, father-and-son duo has collectively wooed Willowbrook crowds for over five decades and are a major factor in its success.

Additional thanks are extended to the following people for their valuable contributions: Chuck Sengstock, author of *That Toddlin' Town* and former public relations person for the Willowbrook Ballroom; Liz Harris, publisher of *Keep Rockin'* magazine; and fiancée Lou Holly, editor. Thanks to Bill Crawford and Cindy Carr for sharing *Willow Springs Crossroads of History*. Appreciation is extended to Don McKenna, director of the Willow Springs historical society, for his impressive knowledge, humor, and willingness to assist. Bravo to our singles dance freelance photographer Steven Fluke, who is featured in the last chapter. Also, a whopping round of applause to John Bonk for his patience, technological wisdom, and assistance in helping me organize an endless pile of photographs. You're the best.

Finally, I thank acquisitions editor Jeff Ruetsche for his patience, encouragement, and belief in this project and me.

INTRODUCTION

The legendary Willowbrook Ballroom (located about 15 miles west of the Chicago loop in the south suburbs of Willow Springs, Illinois) is easily accessible from the 294 East-West tollway or Interstate 55. It has drawn audiences from around the country for fine dining and entertainment. The topography of the Des Plaines River Valley favors Willow Springs as a place of rustic beauty. Known for its chasms, much of what is now Willow Springs is known to geologists as Mt. Forest Island, a sprawling moraine resulting from ancient ice glaciers. The town is said to have been named by DesPlaines River boatmen who stopped to fill water barrels from a magnificent flowing spring that housed a deeply rooted willow tree with water bubbling from beneath the roots. The men so delighted in the beautiful sight during their wearisome journey that they named the area Willow Springs. In existence since 1840, the town is rich in Indian history and was inhabited by the Pottawatomi Indians. Both Archer Avenue and Willow Springs Road were previously Indian trails. The town, also known for its connection to the I&M Canal, maintains a popular bike trail alongside it. Tourists and locals frequent the many acres of forest preserves and picnic groves, the Little Red Schoolhouse and Nature Center (also known as the old, one-room school of School District 116), and an exciting nightlife involving a long list of showstopping entertainers performing at the Willowbrook Ballroom on a weekly basis.

The Willowbrook proudly celebrates its 90th anniversary in 2011. Originally opened in 1921 as an outdoor dance pavilion and picnic grove, it was called Oh Henry Park after the candy bar. It was fully enclosed and enlarged in 1923 due to its tremendous popularity. Destroyed by fire in 1930, the owner, John Verderbar, with a show-must-go-on agenda, hired a crew of 200 carpenters to construct a huge outdoor dance floor. The business opened the following Saturday, attracting record crowds lured by the highly publicized romantic ambiance of dancing under the stars. As hundreds of grand ballrooms sprung up across the nation, dancing became America's top entertainment obsession.

Due to the stellar success of Oh Henry Park, a prestigious Oh Henry Ballroom was constructed less than a year later. Architect William Sevic was a one-time protégé of esteemed architect Harold Zook, who was known for a trademark spiderweb on every building he designed. Sevic had ideas of his own, however, and after being hired as designer of the impressive Oh Henry Ballroom project, he decided to outdo Zook by designing two noticeably larger wrought-iron spiderwebs: one for the lobby and one at the entrance to the Pine Room Lounge.

By the spring of 1931, more than 1,500 dignitaries and invited guests attended the grand opening, with Kenny's Hot Red Peppers entertaining the crowd. A ceiling adorned with massive amounts of silk and cove lighting transformed the room into a riot of colorful, shimmering lights. A trio of elegant chandeliers further illuminated the effect of a floating dance floor that was constructed on cushiony trusses to relieve dancers fatigue. These maple sprung dance floors are specially designed to avoid serious injuries, providing a comfortable surface upon which to waltz and swing.

Intermittently during the 1940s, attendance skyrocketed to a whopping 10,000 people per week, forcing bus services to be rerouted, including those from downtown Chicago to the entrance of the ballroom, in order to accommodate the massive crowds. It was not uncommon to have over 3,500 dancers present in one evening, and another thousand or so were turned away when the venue reached its maximum capacity with folks clamoring to see phenomenal entertainers like Clyde McCoy or Ozzie Nelson and his orchestra.

By the 1950s, an influx of married couples fled from the city to the suburbs. Some of the Chicagoland ballrooms experienced decreased business, and without the benefit of parking lots for the increasing number of automobile owners, some were forced to close. Located in suburbia, Oh Henry Ballroom was able to accommodate patrons with its huge parking lot. The owners also took a risk and built a 20,000-square-foot addition that would feature fine dining in the Willowbrook restaurant, the Carousel Bar, and the Vintage Room, which would be utilized for private banquets. Also included were new, state-of-the-art kitchens.

By 1959, the owners of the increasingly popular dance palace and new restaurant booked well in advance decided to change the Oh Henry name to the Willowbrook Ballroom. Big band headliners—such as Guy Lombardo, Jimmy Dorsey, Harry James, Wayne King, Bob Crosby, and Dick Jurgens—entertained and enchanted hundreds of thousands of enthusiastic ballroom dancers.

During its 90-year history, three generations of Verderbars ran the business for 77 years before current owners Gedaminis and Birute Jodwalis purchased it in 1997. Initially, John Verderbar and his two sons, Rudy and Ed, constructed and ran the operation. And after the three passed away, Ed's wife, Helen Carig Verderbar, stepped into a management role, juggling the tasks of booking bands, negotiating contracts, and supervising a growing staff of employees. To her surprise, booking agents and suppliers were taking bets that the ballroom would fail under her supervision, but this wager served as the impetus for Helen's determination to succeed. Working an exhausting schedule of 12-hour days seven days a week, she succeeded in booking top entertainers like Count Basie, Helen O'Connell, and Sammy Kaye. According to her daughter Patricia ("Pat"), it was Helen who "stepped forward, held on tightly and bridged the past to the future to ultimately save the Willowbrook Ballroom." In the 1980s, Pat, who later married Dick Williams, took over the reins, freeing up Helen so that she could spend time with her grandchildren and baking delectable desserts in the restaurant's kitchens. Dick also worked long hours daily and was involved with updates and renovations. He fostered the idea to hire popular rock bands of the 1960s to liven up the Friday night showcase with nostalgia in the 1980s.

Generation after generation fell in love with the Willowbrook. Although tastes in music have changed, the Verderbars continually reinvented the business with the changing times, developing creative new ideas to draw the crowds. Today, the popular tea and big band ballroom dancing continues to thrive on Sunday afternoons. It is not uncommon for multiple events to take place simultaneously in any number of the five banquet rooms. Dance instructions are offered two nights a week, live entertainers take the stage on other nights, and singles groups dance and mingle to the music of DJs every other Friday. Orchestras, tribute bands, private parties, and numerous other celebrations keep the Willowbrook thriving five nights a week.

Writing this book was a challenge and a labor of love. My mother delighted in dancing to the big band music at the Oh Henry Ballroom decades ago, and today, my friends and I join a new generation of patrons who enjoy socialization and dancing through the singles events or reminiscing with our favorite tribute bands. The images in this book will hopefully lead the reader down a path of historical discovery, depicting a humble outdoor dance pavilion evolving into the exquisite Willowbrook Ballroom—the one remaining ballroom of its magnitude in the Chicagoland area today.

One

THE TOWN OF WILLOW SPRINGS

Shown here is the Dietrich mansion built in 1875 on Charlton Avenue in Willow Springs. Owner Henry Dietrich was a businessman and a colonel in the Civil War. He was the first to build a house on a 300-acre subdivision in Willow Springs, which was then known as Mt. Forest. (Courtesy of Don McKenna.)

The movie *The Package*, a political thriller about an assassination conspiracy involving the military of the United States and Russia, was filmed in Willow Springs. Shown here at the entrance of the Willowbrook Ballroom are actors Gene Hackman and Joanne Cassidy, who starred in the 1989 film. In 2006, *The Lake House*, starring Sandra Bullock and Keanu Reeves, was filmed at Maple Lake. A glass house on stilts was constructed for several scenes but was dismantled after filming was completed. Negotiations were also in the works for the town to serve as the location for *The Fugitive*, however, property owners in Willow Springs could not agree on compensation for use of one of the houses. (Courtesy of Don McKenna.)

The Willowbrook Ballroom parking lot was rented out for a single night to accommodate the trailers of *The Package*'s cast and crew. It also served to house the equipment used in making the film. Some movie scenes took place at the Oh Henry Roadhouse across the street from the ballroom. (Courtesy of Don McKenna.)

The photograph above shows the village hall, police department, and fire department in one building, which was constructed in 1928. The photograph below shows the Springs Forest Deli, which was constructed in 1877. The town of Willow Springs was originally called Springs Forest. (Both courtesy of Don McKenna.)

VIEW OF STORES AND BUSINESS LOCATION ON ARCHER AVENUE, SPRING FOREST, ILL.

The photograph above reflects what the corner of Willow Springs Road and Archer Avenue looked like around 1940. Just west of here stands the Willowbrook Ballroom, which, at that time, was the Oh Henry Ballroom. The photograph below is of the bridge over the I & M Canal located at Charlton Avenue. It was constructed in 1875. (Both courtesy of Don McKenna.)

This is a two-room schoolhouse built in 1913 and named the New Willow Springs public school. In the mid-1930s, additions made it into four rooms, with construction in the 1950s and 1960s converting it into a huge grammar school. The facility was torn down in 2006. (Courtesy of Don McKenna.)

Two

THE VERDERBAR FAMILY AND OH HENRY PARK

Shown here is an original Verderbar family portrait taken in 1931. The family members are, from left to right, (first row) Bertha, wife Margaret, and Mae; (second row) Ed, family patriarch John, and Rudolph, the oldest son. (Courtesy of Pat Williams Verderbar.)

This is the original Oh Henry Park, a woodsy picnic grove and open-air dance pavilion featuring a 40-by-65-foot dance floor, in 1921. It was the first of the Verderbar dance facilities. (Courtesy of Pat Williams Verderbar.)

Original owner John Verderbar and wife Margaret Verderbar (née Schmidt) pose for this family photograph around the 1930s. (Courtesy of Pat Williams Verderbar.)

This building served as the dining area and the original entrance to Oh Henry Park, which was constructed around 1929. (Courtesy of Pat Williams Verderbar.)

Shown here around the 1930s is Rudy Verderbar at the entrance of the Oh Henry Park dance pavilion. This is the original entrance featuring a towering pillar on each side. Note the wrought-iron gate and architectural trademark spiderweb doors that lead the way into the park. Emil Flindt and his orchestra are the entertainment advertised on the marquee above. (Courtesy of Don McKenna.)

Standing in the doorway of the open-air pavilion of Oh Henry Park are Margaret, Ed (with his dog), and John Verderbar. (Courtesy of Pat Williams Verderbar.)

This photograph depicts architect Bill Sevic (left) and friend Ed Verderbar taking a break from a project to share a smoke and a laugh. (Courtesy of Pat Williams Verderbar.)

Oh Henry Park's double-arched entrance is seen here in the early to mid-1920s. This is one of the oldest known photographs of Oh Henry Park before the fire. (Courtesy of Pat Williams Verderbar.)

In this mid-1940s photograph, Rudy and Ed Verderbar saw a tree to clear the land. (Courtesy of Pat Williams Verderbar.)

This photograph taken at the south elevation of the Oh Henry Park in the late 1930s or early 1940s shows a trio of Cadillacs owned by John, Rudy, and Ed Verderbar. It was their vehicle of choice. (Courtesy of Pat Williams Verderbar.)

Featured here is the Oh Henry Park after it was fully enlarged and enclosed. This rustic dance pavilion burned down to the ground on June 26, 1930. (Courtesy of Pat Williams Verderbar.)

John Verderbar is shown laying the cornerstone foundation for the Oh Henry Ballroom in this vintage photograph from the early 1930s. (Courtesy of Pat Williams Verderbar.)

This is the Verderbars' house, which was located on the grounds of Oh Henry Park in the early 1960s. The house was later moved to another location. The architect was Bill Sevic. (Courtesy of Pat Williams Verderbar.)

The young, dark-haired man in the pinstriped suit is Rudy, John Verderbar's oldest and strong-willed son who convinced his father to build Oh Henry Park, foiling the original plan to construct a summer home on the five acres of wooded property. Extremely fond of ballroom dancing, Rudy persisted with relentless nudging until he convinced his father of the winning idea to build the dance pavilion. Rudy passed away in February 1968, just four months after the death of his father in November 1967. (Courtesy of Pat Williams Verderbar.)

The third child of John and Margaret, Bertha Verderbar (now Stadel), is seen here around the 1920s. (Courtesy of Pat Williams Verderbar.)

Shown here around the late 1950s or early 1960s, from left to right, are Rudy Verderbar and his wife, Anne, and Helen and Ed Verderbar. They are having dinner at the popular Willowbrook restaurant, which was often booked several weeks in advance. (Courtesy of Pat Williams Verderbar.)

This photograph was taken in the 1950s and shows, from left to right, Ed Verderbar, Andy Powell (orchestra leader), Elna Fletcher (John Verderbar's long-term housekeeper, nurse, and friend), John Verderbar, Helen Verderbar (Ed's wife), and Dolly Powell (Andy's wife). They are enjoying a night of dining and dancing at the Willowbrook. (Courtesy of Pat Williams Verderbar.)

This photograph taken in the late 1940s or early 1950s depicts a meeting of the Willow Springs Businessmen's Association at Kegl's Restaurant. Sitting at the table, second and seventh from left, respectively, are Rudy Rampage, owner of Standard Station, and Ed Verderbar. Also at the table are Tony Kegl (first from right); barber James Sturgeon (third from right); Leonard Coombs (fifth from right), owner of Royal Blue Grocery; and Henry Koller of Banks & Koller Tavern is to Coombs's right. In back to the right of the valence is Lee Reynolds, who became fire chief. Other attendees are unidentified. (Courtesy of Pat Williams Verderbar.)

In March 1949, Edward Verderbar received this certification of membership in the Business and Professional Men's Association of Willow Springs. (Courtesy of Birute Jodwalis.)

Business and Professional Men's Association
of Willow Springs, Illinois

THIS IS TO CERTIFY THAT

Edward Verderbar

is a member in good standing of the Business and Professional Men's Association of Willow Springs, a non-profit, non-political organization founded for the purpose of encouraging the growth and development of the village, promoting good will and understanding among the members and supporting all worth-while community activities.

James B Hanlon
President

Earl F. Marshall
Secretary

For the year ending March 1949

Helen Verderbar (née Carig), wife of Ed Verderbar, stands in front of a mural on the wall of Argo State Bank. It was one in a landmarks series covering the Southwest area. Shown in the upper right-hand corner is the Willowbrook Ballroom. (Courtesy of Pat Williams Verderbar.)

In this image, the Verderbar family celebrates John's 90th birthday at what was then called the Willowbrook Room in January 1966. Pictured are, from left to right, Anne, Helen, Ed, Mickey, Pat, Rudy, and John Verderbar. The following year, John's 91st birthday was featured in the January 1967 issue of Enterprise Publications' *Midweek Family Magazine*, which focused on 45 years of success in the entertainment industry. (Courtesy of Pat Williams Verderbar.)

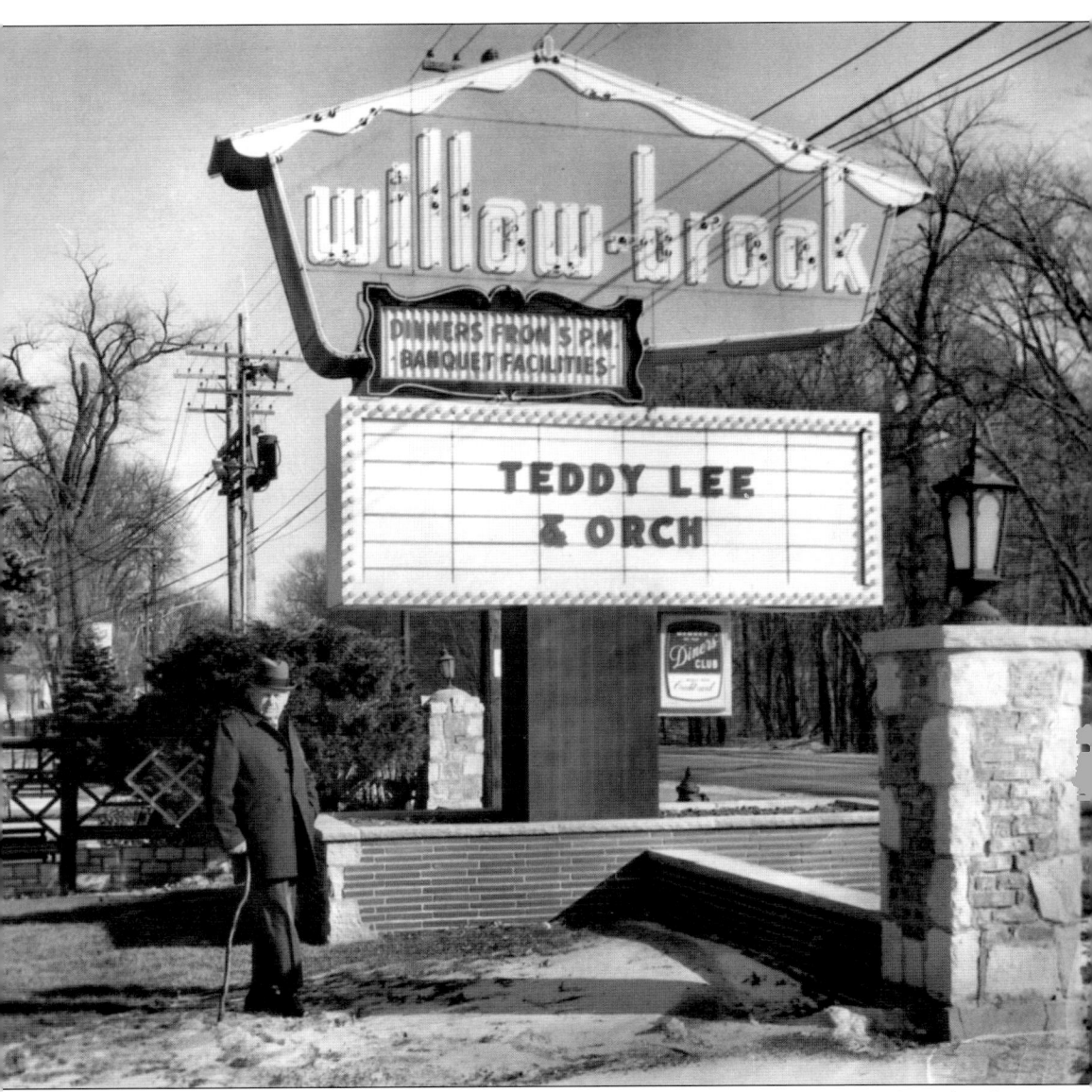

John Verderbar, founder and original owner of the Willowbrook Ballroom, stands under the Willowbrook marquee one bright afternoon in the early 1960s. He is leaning on the cane his son Ed had fashioned for him from crab apple tree. A favorite entertainer and close friend of the Verderbar family, Teddy Lee and his orchestra are advertised as entertainment for that week. A closer look reveals a partial view of a 1956 Buick driving down Archer Avenue. Verderbar was a hardworking nature lover who believed in God. He barely escaped a horrific coal mining accident in Michigan's Upper Peninsula before finding success in the insurance and real estate business prior to building Oh Henry Park–turned–Willowbrook. (Courtesy of Pat Williams Verderbar.)

A live 20-foot-tall Christmas tree was an annual holiday tradition since 1955 and drew its share of spectators. It towered near the entrance of the dance floor for everyone to view as they entered the ballroom. In the late 1970s, an artificial tree of equal stature was used in place of a real one, and each year, the spectacular tree stands tall and adorned with huge ornaments and colorful, enticing packages placed beneath it. (Courtesy of Pat Williams Verderbar.)

From left to right, orchestra leader and family friend Teddy Lee Sr. poses with Helen Carig Verderbar, famed jazz pianist Count Basie, and Pat Williams Verderbar around the 1980s. (Courtesy of Pat Williams Verderbar.)

This family photograph was taken in the Bordeaux Room of the Willowbrook Ballroom in 1994 in honor of Alivia Williams's First Communion. Pictured from left to right are Dick Williams, Alivia Carlotta Williams (kneeling), Pat Williams Verderbar, Lisa Sistos Williams (standing), and Claire Helena Williams. (Courtesy of Pat Williams Verderbar.)

Shown here are Dick Williams and Pat Williams Verderbar with their daughters Alivia (left) and Claire. They are dressed for a New Year's Eve celebration at the Willowbrook. (Courtesy of Pat Williams Verderbar.)

This is the Williams family on the night the Willowbrook won the Illinois Family Business of the Year Award in 1996. It was just a year before the business was sold to current owners Gedas and Birute Jodwalis, with the assurance that the establishment would maintain its original tradition of fine dining and dancing to the best music in entertainment. From left to right are Dick Williams, Pat Williams Verderbar, Lisa Sistos Williams, and (in front) Alivia and Claire Williams. (Courtesy of Pat Williams Verderbar.)

Three

ORCHESTRAS AND BIG BANDS (THE EARLY DAYS)

This is a montage of an old ticket stub, an advertisement, and photographs with views of both the inside and outside of the legendary Oh Henry Ballroom. (Courtesy of Birute Jodwalis.)

Here is a photograph of the famous Ray Pearl Orchestra in 1953. The traveling band played successfully from coast to coast, and Pearl was sought after by major movie studios. It is said that a feud between Pearl and the artist's union ended his career in 1956. Teddy Lee Sr. played with Pearl for a decade, arranging music and directing the band, in addition to playing the saxophone. Lee formed his own band with some of the members of the Ray Pearl band, and it was an immediate success. (Courtesy of Teddy Lee Jr.)

Shown here, from left to right, are Ray Pearl, his cousin Betty Kelly, and Bill Darlow. Ray called Betty "Lady Cotton Patch Cinderella." (Courtesy of Teddy Lee Jr.)

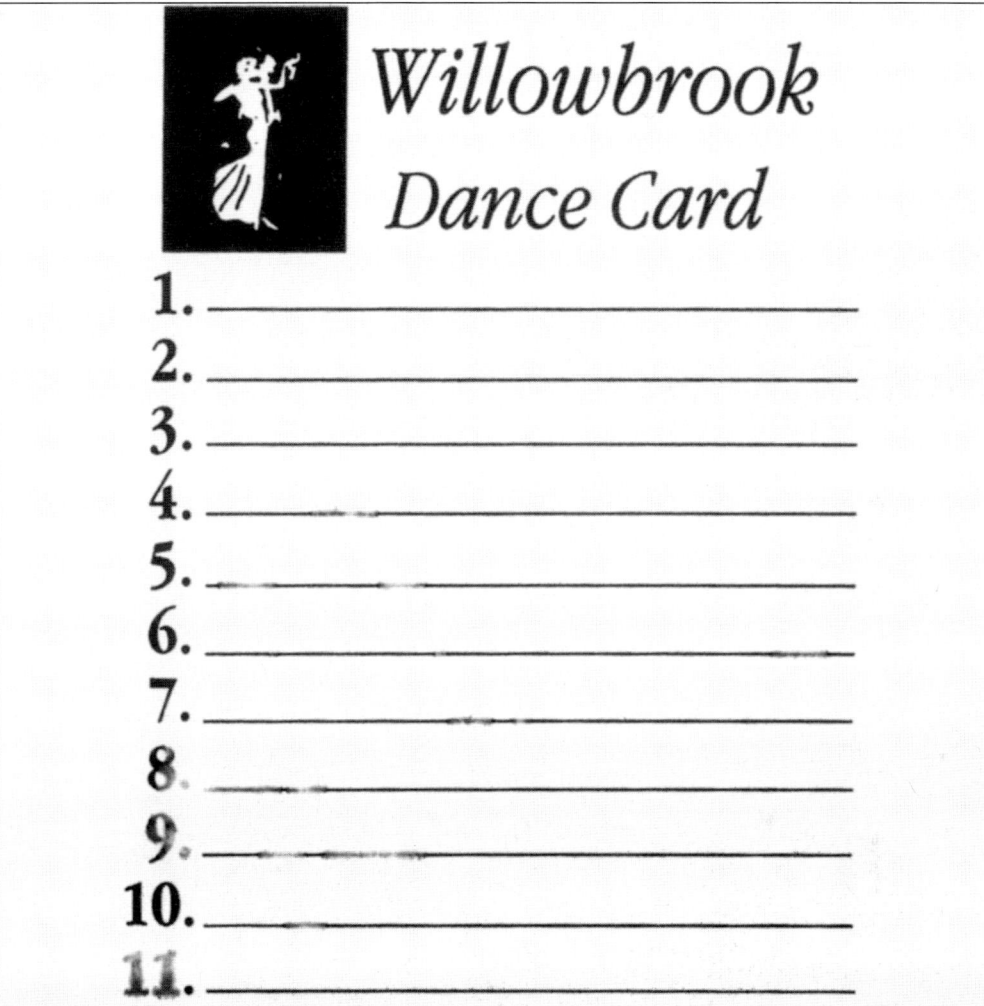

Willowbrook
Dance Card

1. _____
2. _____
3. _____
4. _____
5. _____
6. _____
7. _____
8. _____
9. _____
10. _____
11. _____

During the early days when the Willowbrook was still called the Oh Henry, a 10¢-a-dance card was implemented. Ladies would use this type of card to line up dances for the evening. The term "my dance card is full" is sometimes still used today as an expression that the lady or gentleman plans to or has promised to dance with a variety of different partners. The Charleston, the shimmy, the waltz, the fox-trot, and the swing were some of the popular dances back then, but the shimmy was later condemned as sinful. (Courtesy of Birute Jodwalis.)

Oh Henry

FOUNTAIN MENU

The front and back of the Oh Henry fountain menu from the 1940s features a shot of the Oh Henry Ballroom and the courtyard gardens where many dancers came out for fresh air or romantic walks in the moonlight. Many proposals also took place here. (Both courtesy of Eric Bronsky.)

OPEN ALL YEAR

FOUNTAIN SPECIALS

SPECIAL SUNDAE

Special

Chocolate Pecan Sundae

40c

SUNDAES

Chocolate	30	Hot Fudge	30
Pineapple	30	Marshmallow	. . .30
Strawberry	. . .30	Butterscotch	30
	Cherry 30		

Pecans 10c Extra

SODAS

Chocolate	30	Root Beer	30
Pineapple	30	Green River	. . .30
Strawberry	. . .30	Vanilla	30
	Cherry 30		

DELICIOUS DRINKS

MALTED MILKS

Chocolate	30	Cherry	30
Pineapple	30	Vanilla	30
Strawberry	. . .30	Root Beer	30

FRESH FRUIT DRINKS

Fresh Orange	. . .30	Grape Juice	30
Fresh Lime	. . .30	Fresh Lemon	. . .30

BEVERAGES

Coca Cola	20	Lemon	20
Root Beer	20	Cherry	20
	Green River 20		

Visit the Marine Room Downstairs for

Beverages and Tasty Sandwiches

SERVING MEADOW GOLD ICE CREAM

The inside of the same menu shows the modest prices of cold beverages and ice-cream desserts during the 1940s, when people could purchase a car for $800, a house for $6,500, and fill up a gas tank at 18¢ a gallon. (Courtesy of Eric Bronsky.)

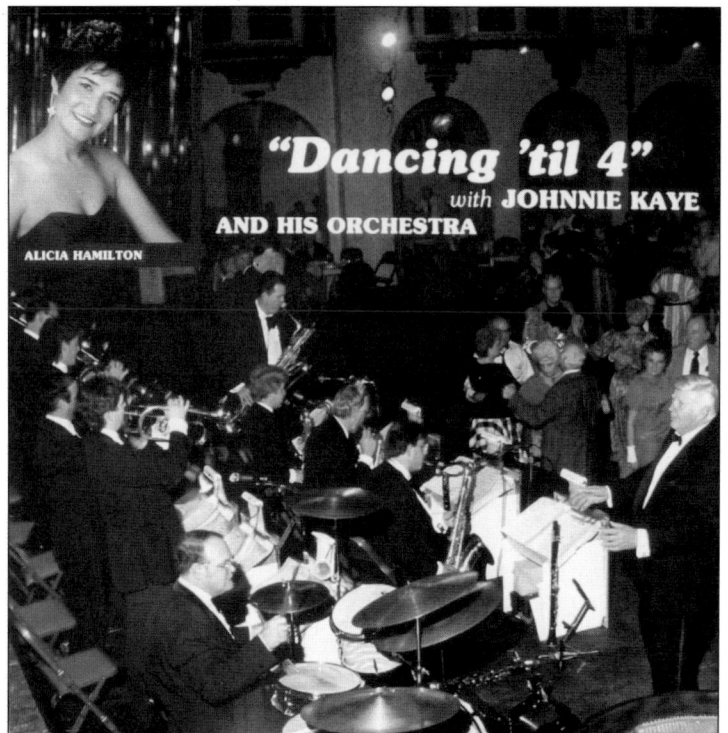

This Johnnie Kaye promotional photograph shows Johnnie with his orchestra and longtime vocalist Alicia Hamilton, a member of the band for over 25 years. This photograph was taken around 1987. (Courtesy of Dan Stevens.)

Orchestra leader Johnnie Kaye led a 13-piece band for 63 years. He played piano and accordion since childhood but later picked up his baton to lead the band. Kaye passed away in 2010, just two days before his 85th birthday. He was married to his wife Rita for 60 years. He and his band played frequently at the Willowbrook and other venues in the Midwest, in addition to performing on several cruise ships. The band members were known to appear in formal attire, often sporting tuxedoes. (Courtesy of Dan Stevens.)

Alicia Hamilton stands next to Johnnie Kaye in this group photograph. Some identified members include drummer Brian Weber and trumpet player Vince Gelsomino (seen in the middle of the three trumpeters), a member of the band for over 30 years. Chuck Cunningham was also a trumpet player with the band for 17 years. (Courtesy of Dan Stevens.)

Don Dygert, a trumpet player with the Teddy Lee Orchestra for over 30 years, points to the famous bandleader wall that was previously on display at the Willowbrook's Piano Bar Lounge. The walls have been painted over and are currently covered with framed celebrity photographs and other memorabilia. This c. 1970s photograph shows only a portion of the wall celebrating some of the great legends that performed over the years. (Courtesy of Teddy Lee Jr.)

Buddy Rich was billed as the world's greatest drummer. Amazingly, he seemed destined to play drums, as it is said that he started tapping spoons at the early age of one, performed on Broadway at four, and was a bandleader at age 11. According to other musicians, he played jazz, big band, and swing music "with a speed, style, and execution that were next to impossible to duplicate." The self-taught drummer received numerous awards and honors and gained international recognition for his 10-minute *West Side Story* medley. His music career spanned seven decades, and his well-known associations included top performers Artie Shaw, Tommy Dorsey, Harry James, Les Brown, Nat King Cole, Frank Sinatra, Ella Fitzgerald, and Louis Armstrong. Rich was a regular on talk shows, including the *Tonight Show* and the *Merv Griffin Show*. He also performed for former presidents, including Franklin Roosevelt, John F. Kennedy, and Ronald Reagan. (Courtesy of Brute Jodwalis.)

Chuck Foster's orchestra boasted three trumpets, one trombone, three saxophones (including himself), and three rhythms. Foster, who also played the clarinet, started his band in the late 1930s and played around the Midwest dance circuit in the 1950s. He was still growing strong in the late 1970s and 1980s, playing ballrooms, such as the Willowbrook. Some of his long-term band members were Don Crawford (trumpeter), Dick Arant (trombonist), Bill Gee (lead alto saxophone), Wayne Harden (tenor saxophone), Jimmy Castle (singer and saxophone player), Hal Pruden (pianist), Stewart Strange (bassist), Bob Simpson (drummer), and vocalists Dorothy Bradon or Dottie Dotson. (Courtesy of Pat Williams Verderbar.)

Teddy Lee Sr. and his orchestra are dazzling the sellout crowd at a Willowbrook New Year's Eve party. Teddy Lee Jr. still plays regularly at holiday events and is one of the most popular draws to the ballroom on Sunday afternoons. Both previous and current owners attest that they are a huge part of the venue's success due to their huge fan base, engaging personalities, and favored compositions. Original owner John Verderbar was particularly fond of Teddy Lee Sr., as were all of his fans. (Courtesy of Teddy Lee Jr.)

This is one of the earliest photographs of the Teddy Lee Orchestra in 1959. Teddy Lee Sr. is the fourth saxophone on the left. Other musicians are unidentified. (Courtesy of Charles C. Sengstock.)

Henry Lega, also known as Teddy Lee Sr., toured nationally, but his big break came when he joined Ray Pearl. This solitary picture of Teddy Lee Sr. was taken in the 1950s. His orchestra was formed in 1959. The orchestra mixed it up with big band favorites, swing, Latin, and jazz. (Courtesy of Teddy Lee Jr.)

This photograph of Teddy Lee Sr. was taken at the Willowbrook in the 1960s and shows a partial shot of the orchestra. Lee was one of the big-name orchestras in Chicagoland, with a loyal following for decades. In 1990, after 55 years in business, son Ted Lega (also known as Teddy Lee Jr.) took over the band, which continues to thrive. (Courtesy of Teddy Lee Jr.)

Two great orchestra leaders and friends are shown here, posing for a photograph at the Willowbrook. Teddy Lee Sr. is on the left, and Wayne King is on the right. (Courtesy of Charles C. Sengstock.)

Teddy Lee Sr.'s signed promotional photograph hangs on the wall of the Willowbrook office, along with dozens of other great entertainers. The music was referred to as "Music Sweet with a Beat." (Courtesy of Birute Jodwalis.)

This is Teddy Lee Jr. in 1992. He began playing piano at age eight, after which he learned the clarinet and saxophone. By the age of 19, he was teaching and performing. He and his father played together at thousands of engagements. Teddy Jr. was inducted into the distinguished American Bandmasters Association. (Courtesy of Teddy Lee Jr.)

The dance floor was packed at this mid-1980s New Year's Eve party at the Willowbrook. Teddy Lee Sr. is shown in the black suit with his back to the camera. The woman next to him is thought to be Ms. Weiss. (Courtesy of Teddy Lee Jr.)

Teddy Lee Sr. leads the orchestra once again at an outdoor venue around the 1990s. (Courtesy of Teddy Lee Jr.)

Teddy Lee Sr. leads the orchestra while an unidentified vocalist performs sometime in the 1990s. (Courtesy of Teddy Lee Jr.)

This Oh Henry Ballroom postcard is from 1944. It highlights the dance floor, seen in the upper right, as well as the finely landscaped grounds of the venue. (Courtesy of Birute Jodwalis.)

This is a 1960s Willowbrook postcard depicting a photograph of the Oh Henry Ballroom as it appeared in 1938. (Courtesy of Brute Jodwalis.)

This Willowbrook postcard shows the Willowbrook Room and the Piano Bar as it once looked, seen on the bottom, from left to right. On the top, the Willowbrook marquee (left) and the Camelot Room are shown. Each room was eventually renovated, and the names were changed. (Courtesy of Birute Jodwalis.)

Buddy Morrow was a bandleader, trombonist, arranger, and composer from 1933 until his death in 2010. He was the conductor of the Tommy Dorsey Orchestra for decades and a member of the *Tonight Show* band during the 1960s. In 2009, just a year before his death, he was awarded the prestigious International Trombone Association's Lifetime Achievement Award. His early-1950s recordings "Rose, Rose, I Love You" and "Night Train" appeared on US billboard charts. Morrow also played with greats like Harry James, Buddy Rich, and Jimmy Dorsey. (Courtesy of Brute Jodwalis.)

The Pete Duchin Orchestra shown here was started in 1962 but was originally led by Pete's father, Eddy, in the 1930s. Pete is a pianist, conductor, and composer who played at the Willowbrook Ballroom's 60th anniversary celebration in 1981 and at exclusive events, such as political conventions, charity benefits, and weddings—including the weddings of Arnold Schwarzenegger and Maria Shriver and Sarah Jessica Parker and Matthew Broderick. Pete also served as musical coordinator for Pres. Lyndon Johnson's inauguration. The story of Pete's parents, Eddy Duchin and Marjorie Oelriche, is depicted in a 1956 movie called *The Eddy Duchin Story*, starring Tyrone Powers and Kim Novak. Pete is known for over 26 recordings. (Courtesy of Birute Jodwalis.)

The Vito Buffalo Orchestra was a 10-piece band that Vito led for more than 40 years. Playing trumpet, singing, and entertaining audiences with his impersonations of Louis Armstrong, Frank Sinatra, and Tony Bennett, Vito was billed as a unique and talented favorite of the huge crowds he drew into the ballroom. (Courtesy of Birute Jodwalis.)

The late Count Basie was a famous jazz pianist and big band leader during the swing era for almost 50 years, beginning in 1935. Basie played in Bennie Moten's band and later led a band called the Barons of Rhythm. The band's theme song was "The One O'clock Jump," and it was inducted into the Grammy Hall of Fame. He played at the Willowbrook during his early career in the 1940s and returned in the later years of his career for special appearances. (Courtesy of Birute Jodwalis.)

Helen O'Connell signed up with Jimmy Dorsey in 1938, teaming up for songs like "Green Eyes" and "Tangerine." In 1950, she embarked on a solo career, making occasional records and appearing on television shows. She later appeared with Jimmy Dorsey's ghost band after his death. She also appeared in a few films in the 1940s. O'Connell was a welcome act at the Willowbrook Ballroom. (Courtesy of Birute Jodwalis.)

Ray McKinley was one of the top drummers, singers, and bandleaders during the swing era. Before World War II, he played with Jimmy Dorsey and, later, with the Glenn Miller Orchestra. For a period of time, he formed his own band and also worked as a television singer in New York City. McKinley was married to Peggy Lennon of the singing group the Lennon Sisters, who appeared regularly on the *Lawrence Welk Show*. (Courtesy of Birute Jodwalis.)

ARTIE SHAW

Artie Shaw earned a reputation as one of jazz's finest clarinet players He was also a composer, bandleader, and writer of fiction and nonfiction, including a semiautobiographical book, *The Trouble with Cinderella*. He performed with many bands and orchestras during his career, and in addition to signing on Buddy Rich as drummer, he is remembered for signing Billie Holiday in 1938, becoming the first white bandleader to hire a full-time black female singer as part of his orchestra prior to touring the segregated South. He was dubbed the "King of Swing," and his recording "Begin the Beguine" is said to be one of the hottest selling records in history. His multiple marriages included actresses Ava Gardner and Lana Turner as wives, with his marriage to Evelyn Keyes being his longest. (Courtesy of Birute Jodwalis.)

Norm Ladd was born Norbert Hladilek and was an alto saxophone and clarinet player with popular big bands, starting in the 1950s. He played at the Willowbrook Ballroom for over three decades until his death in his Rolling Meadows home in 1999. The orchestra leader brought in close to a thousand dancers during the ballroom's Sunday afternoon festivities. (Courtesy of Birute Jodwalis.)

Jack Morgan began playing trombone at the age of 13. He joined his father Russ Morgan's orchestra at 17 years old, after he overheard a phone call that his father's first trombonist couldn't make it one night. Jack performed alongside his dad at that engagement and for another decade. He took over the band after his father's death in 1969. Jack was multilingual and was capable of singing in several different languages. The outstanding musician earned five gold records and was inducted into the Big Band Hall of Fame in 1997. The Russ Morgan Orchestra, with Jack still at the realm, celebrated its 75th anniversary in 2010. (Courtesy of Birute Jodwalis.)

Four

ROCK BANDS FROM THE 1960S AND 1970S

The Buckinghams originated in the Chicago area in 1966 and soared to the top of the charts less than a year later. Original members included: Carl Giammiarese, Nick Fortuna, Marty Grebb, Dennis Tufano, and John Paulos. *Billboard Magazine* once referred to them as "the most listened to band in America." The band impressed their fans continuously with No. 1 hit "Kind of a Drag," No. 11 hit "Susan," No. 6 hit "Don't You Care," and No. 5 hit "Mercy, Mercy, Mercy." The band split in the 1970s but made a comeback in the 1980s, continuing to draw crowds throughout the country with their nostalgic songs performed at concerts and festivals. (Courtesy of Birute Jodwalis.)

PERFORMING THEIR HITS:
"Kind of a Drag"
"Don't You Care"
"Mercy, Mercy, Mercy"
"Hey Baby, They're Playing Our Song"
"Susan"

TOMMY ROE

Tommy Roe was another of many artists who found fame in the 1960s. He played the Willowbrook in the 1980s as part of their oldies shows. Roe had six top-10 hits during the 1960s, including "Sheila" and "Dizzy," which both reached No. 1 on the billboard chart. In 1986, he was inducted into the Georgia Music Hall of Fame. Other songs he is recognized for are "Jam Up and Jelly Tight," "Sweet Pea," and "Hooray for Hazel." (Courtesy of Birute Jodwalis.)

This group picture of the Coasters was taken in 1987. The original members who started the doo-wop rock 'n' roll group in the mid-1950s included Carl Gardner, Billy Guy, Bobby Nunn, Leon Hughes, Young Jessie, and Adolph Jacobs, who left the group in 1959. Their greatest hits were "Yakety Yak," "Charlie Brown," and "Poison Ivy." (Courtesy of Birute Godwalis.)

THE COASTERS

Chubby Checker

Chubby Checker was born Ernest Evans in 1941. An American singer and songwriter, he popularized the song that became a dancing sensation, "The Peppermint Twist." His follow-up song ,"Let's Twist Again," won a Grammy award for Best Rock 'n' Roll Solo Performance. Another major hit, "Limbo Rock," reached No. 2 on the charts, and partygoers and dancers lined up to shimmy under a limbo stick that was positioned lower and lower, making it more challenging to win and almost impossible to get under the stick without knocking it off its stand. Checker had five albums in the top 12 simultaneously, a feat no other recording artist had achieved. (Courtesy of Birute Jodwalis.)

Gary Lewis, of Gary Lewis and the Playboys' fame, was another 1960s rock band that drew sellout crowds to the Willowbrook Ballroom in the 1980s. The band's accomplishments included 45 million records sold worldwide, 17 top-40 hits, 10 gold singles, and four gold albums. "This Diamond Ring" soared to the top of the charts, as did "Count Me In." Other top-10 hits included "Save Your Heart For Me," "Everybody Loves a Clown," "She's Just My Style," and "Sure Gonna Miss Her." Gary was the first and only artist to have his first seven releases reach the top 10 on the Hot 100 Chart. The band appeared on *American Bandstand*, the *Ed Sullivan Show*, and the *Tonight Show*. Gary was the son of famed comedian and actor Jerry Lewis. (Courtesy of Birute Jodwalis.)

RARE EARTH

Northern International
2345 Eifert Road
HOLT, MICHIGAN 48842
(517) 694-3400

Rare Earth, like most rock bands, made frequent changes in members who came and went over the years. The original members were Gil Bridges, Pete Rivera (Hoorelbeke), John Persh (Parrish), Rod Richards (Rod Cox), and Kenny James (Ken Folcik). The band joined Motown in 1969 and received recognition for smash hits like "Get Ready" and "I Just Want to Celebrate." (Courtesy of Birute Jodwalis.)

Rhythm and blues singer Otis Day (DeWayne Jessie) was a vocalist and actor who starred in *National Lampoon's Animal House* in 1978, a movie in which Otis Day and the Knights perform two songs: "Shout" and "Shama Lama Ding Dong." Jessie, who changed his name to Otis Day, was also knows for his cinematic roles in *Car Wash* and *Thank God It's Friday.* He performed his hits at the Willowbrook as part of the oldies acts on Friday nights. (Courtesy of Birute Jodwalis.)

Rhythm, blues, and pop artist Martha Reeves sang lead for Motown's Martha and the Vandellas (Rosalind Ashford and Betty Kelly), scoring huge hits with enormously popular songs like "Jimmy Mack," "Dancing in the Streets," and "Nowhere to Run." Although the group disbanded, Martha made a few solo appearances at venues like the Willowbrook Ballroom. In 1995, Martha and the Vandellas were inducted into the Rock and Roll Hall of Fame. Reeves also penned a best-selling autobiography titled *Dancing in the Street*. The politically oriented Reeves also served as a councilwoman in the city of Detroit. (Courtesy of Birute Jodwalis.)

THE CRYAN' SHAMES

The Cryan' Shames performed at the Willowbrook Ballroom's 75th anniversary celebration in 1996. The 1960s to 1970s band was known for monster hits like "Sugar and Spice," "I Wanna Meet You," "Mr. Unreliable," "Could Be We're in Love," and "Up on the Roof." The group disbanded for a short time and reunited in the 1980s. Founding member Jim Pilster, who played the Latin percussion, cymbal kicks and vocals, and Tom Doody, the original lead singer, are the remaining original members. Additional members include Rocky Penn (drums and vocals), Greg Brucker (bass guitar and vocals), and Michael Ayres (percussion and vibes). The Cryan' Shames bear the distinction of being the first Chicago rock group to sing and record with a major record label; they signed with Columbia. The band currently appears at local fests and venues, with enthusiastic fans singing along as they venture down memory lane. (Courtesy of Birute Jodwalis.)

The *Vogues*

KEN HILL
PRODUCTIONS. INC
772 Zubel Road
Apollo, PA 15613-9617
(412) 727-3488

The original members of the Vogues included Bill Burkette (lead baritone), Don Miller (baritone), Hugh Geyer (first tenor), and Chuck Blasko (second tenor). Two of the group's most memorable hits were "You're the One" and "Five O'clock World," which later became the theme for the *Drew Carey Show*. The Vogues were another band that joined the Friday night lineup of nostalgic entertainers. (Courtesy of Birute Jodwalis.)

CHIPPENDALES on the "DOLLY PARTON SHOW"—ABC

Dolly Parton was a big attraction and one of the many Friday night artists who performed at the Willowbrook in the 1980s. She is also the owner of Dollywood, an amusement park in Gatlinburg, Tennessee, where many great country stars have performed on stage in theaters and outdoor pavilions. The multitalented country singer, songwriter, actress, author, philanthropist, and musician is frequently referred to as the "Queen of Country Music." The diva had three No. 1 hits in a row: "Starting Over Again," "Old Flames Can't Hold a Candle to You," and "Nine to Five," which was the theme song for the hit movie of the same name that she starred in with Jane Fonda and Lily Tomlin. Later, she lit up the big screen in *Straight Talk* with actor James Woods. (Courtesy of Birute Jodwalis.)

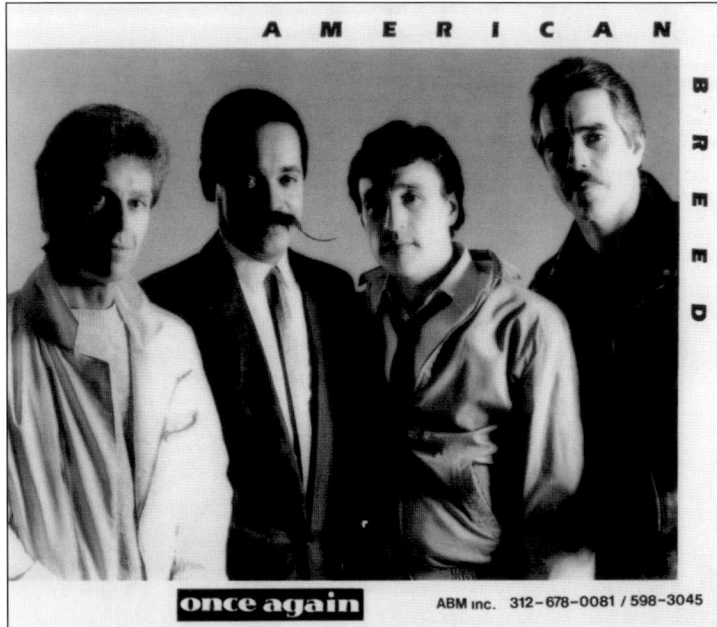

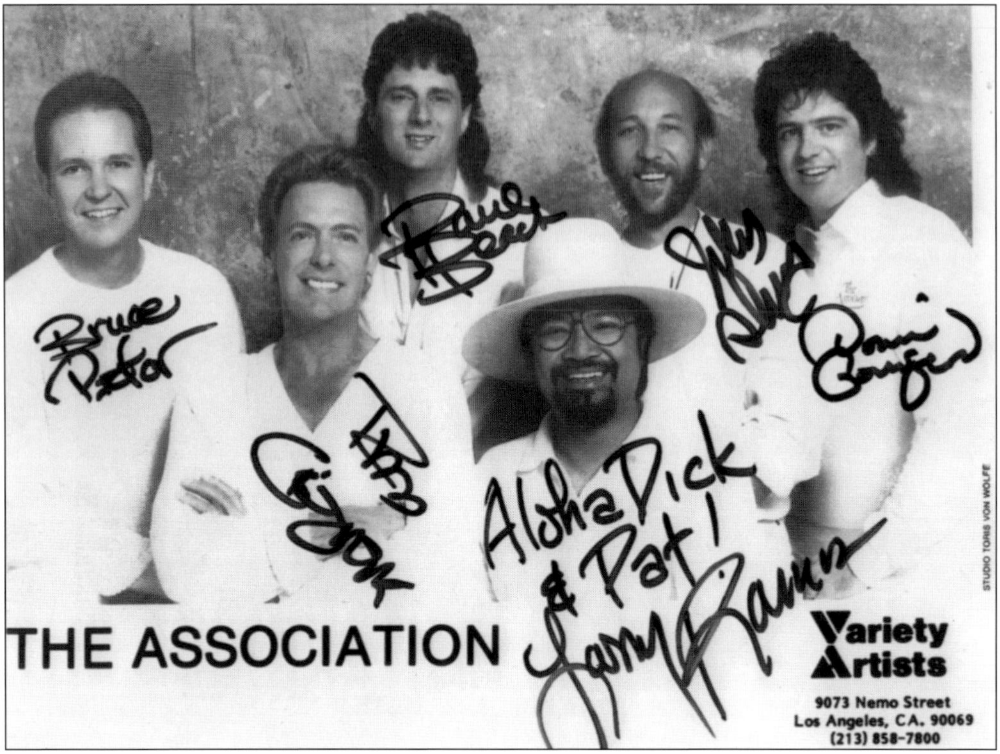
THE ASSOCIATION
Aloha Dick & Pat!
Variety Artists
9073 Nemo Street
Los Angeles, CA. 90069
(213) 858-7800

The Association's greatest tunes included "Along Comes Mary," "Cherish," "Windy," and "Never My Love." The original lineup of members were Jules Gary Alexander, Terry Kirkman, Brian Cole, Russ Giguere, and Ted Bluechel Jr. Bob Page was briefly a member until he was replaced by Jim Yester. The band was only together a few years but made quite an impact with a mellow mix of major hits. (Courtesy of Brute Jodwalis.)

AMERICAN
BREED
once again
ABM inc. 312-678-0081 / 598-3045

The rock band American Breed formed in Cicero, Illinois, originally as Gary and the Nite Lites. Their biggest hit, "Bend Me Shape Me," reached No. 5 on the US Billboard Hot 100 Chart in 1968. The group appeared on Dick Clark's *American Bandstand* but split in 1969. The original members were Gary Loizzo (vocalist), Al Ciner (guitar), Lee Graziano (drums), and Chuck Colbert (bass). (Courtesy of Birute Jodwalis.)

The Guess Who were superstars in Canada and were known for several megahits in the US, such as "American Woman," "These Eyes," and "Share the Land." Original members included Chad Allan, Randy Bachman, Jim Kale, Bob Ashley, and Gary Peterson. (Courtesy of Birute Jodwalis.)

Danny and the Juniors emerged in 1955 as a doo-wop group, including Danny Rapp, Dave White, Frank Maffei, and Joe Terranova. The group found favor with audiences with hits like "At the Hop" and "Rock and Roll Is Here to Stay." In the years following Danny Rapp's tragic death, Danny and the Juniors performed with Joe Jerry at the Willowbrook in the 1980s. (Courtesy of Birute Jodwalis.)

MANAGEMENT: HOWARD SILVERMAN
DAVID FISHOF PRODUCTIONS, INC.
888 SEVENTH AVE. SUITE 402
NY NY 10019 (212) 757-1605

VILLAGE PEOPLE

TCI TALENT CONSULTANTS INTERNATIONAL Ltd.

The unmistakable Village People were another entertainment sensation that took stage at the Willowbrook dance mecca. Famous for hit songs like "YMCA," "In the Navy," and "Macho Man," the Village People won many awards, including Favorite Musical Group in 1979. Band members have included Felipe Rose, an original member who plays the role of a Native American; Alex Briley, an original member who sports the soldier's uniform; and David Hodo, original member who dresses as a construction worker. Ray Simpson has portrayed the police officer since 1979. Jeff Olson joined as the cowboy in 1980, and Eric Anzalone replaced original member Glenn Hughes as the biker in 1995. At the height of their success, the Village People appeared on television shows, including *The Love Boat*, The *Bob Hope Show*, *20/20*, and *American Bandstand*. (Courtesy of Birute Jodwalis.)

ATLANTIC RECORDING ARTISTS

The Shadows of Knight

Performing Their #1 Hit: G-L-O-R-I-A

Management By:
Ultimate Productions, Inc.
2521 Ridge Rd.
Lansing, IL 60432
(312) 895-1925
Personal Management: John Schmidt

Photo Credit: PRESS PHOTO

The Shadows of Knight were another famous 1960s rock band from the Chicago suburbs. Founding members are Warren Rogers (lead guitar and vocals), Roger Spielman (rhythm and lead guitar), Norm Gotsch (rhythm guitar), Wayne Pursull (bass guitar), Tom Schiffour (drums), and Jim Sohns (vocals.) Their biggest hit, "Gloria," sold over eight million copies. Their last hit song, "Shake," sold another million copies. (Courtesy of Birute Jodwalis.)

The Diamonds were a 1950s to 1960s rock group featuring original members Dave Somerville (lead), Ted Kowalski (tenor), Phil Levitt (baritone), and Bill Reed (bass). Most memorable hits were "Little Darlin' " in 1957 and "The Stroll" in 1958. By 1961, all original members left the group, but almost four decades later, they reunited to perform on "Do-Wop 51" in 2000 and, later, a PBS production entitled *Magic Moments—the Best of '50s Pop* in 2004. (Courtesy of Birute Jodwalis.)

Willowbrook entertainer Al Pierson—an accomplished musician, composer, arranger, vocalist, and bandleader—taught music at colleges in Illinois. Over a decade after Guy Lombardo's death, Al Pierson took up his baton and revived Guy Lombardo's Royal Canadians in 1989. Pierson and the Royal Canadians gained tremendous acclaim throughout the United States and Canada, and for many years, Pierson was broadcasted on PBS. Dubbed as Mr. Personality, he received the honor of being named in "Who's Who in Entertainment" and was nominated to the highest acclaim of "Who's Who in The World." (Courtesy of Birute Jodwalis.)

Five

BACK TO THE GREAT ORCHESTRAS

This Wayne King photograph was taken at the Willowbrook Ballroom in 1977, though he also made appearances there in the 1960s. Here, he leans over to talk to one of his many fans. Originally from Illinois, King created Wayne King and His Orchestra in 1927, when he was only 26 years old. The saxophone player, songwriter, singer, and orchestra leader was often referred to as the "Waltz King." (Courtesy of Mike Stosich.)

Shown at the same performance in 1977, Wayne King plays the saxophone while sporting a jacket and tie. (Courtesy of Mike Stosich.)

Another Wayne King photograph shows him performing at the Willowbrook in 1977. His first recording in 1929 was "To Be Forgotten." Other familiar recordings are "Dream a Little Dream of Me," a No. 1 hit, and "Maria Elena," a No. 2 hit. (Courtesy of Mike Stosich.)

This is Wayne King's promotional photograph taken around the 1980s, where he poses in a white jacket and signs his name sweetened with words of warmth to owners Helen Carig Verderbar and Pat Williams Verderbar. (Courtesy of Birute Jodwalis.)

This photograph of Tex Benecke was taken at a 1979 performance at the Willowbrook Ballroom. A talented saxophonist, singer, and bandleader, he is shown here waving to his fans. Benecke was associated with the Glenn Miller Orchestra in the late 1930s and early 1940s. After Miller's disappearance during the war, Benecke lead the orchestra and later formed his own band with a similar style. Benecke made appearances on famed talk shows, such as *The Tonight Show* with Johnny Carson and The *Merv Griffin Show*. He received a star on the Hollywood Walk of Fame in 1992 and died in 2000. (Courtesy of Mike Stosich.)

Shown here at the same 1979 performance, Tex Benecke takes a break from playing the saxophone so that he can sing to the audience. (Courtesy of Mike Stosich.)

Sammy Kaye, seen here with his orchestra as he plays the clarinet in 1978 at the Willowbrook Ballroom, is the second male from the left. Kaye also played the saxophone and made a large number of records with big-name labels during the big band era. His well-known quote was "swing and sway with Sammy Kaye." (Courtesy of Mike Stosich.)

After the Pearl Harbor attack, Kaye wrote the music for *Remember Pearl Harbor*. His radio show was interrupted by the announcement of the attack. Singers were Don Cornell, Barry Frank, Nancy Norman, Tommy Ryan, Gary Wilner, and Billy Williams. Band members were Dale Cornell, Ralph Flangan, Marty Oscard, and Sid Rhein. (Courtesy of Mike Stosich.)

This is another 1978 photograph of Sammy Kaye. He took such pleasure in audience involvement that, during his performances, he called fans on stage to let them conduct the band. He would start the hilarious segment by asking, "So you want to lead the band?" (Courtesy of Mike Stosich.)

Shown here is one last 1978 photograph of Sammy Kaye with unidentified orchestra members. In 1992, Kaye was posthumously inducted into the Big Band and Jazz Hall of Fame. After his death in 1987, his orchestra carried on under the leadership of trumpet player Roger Thorpe, and they continue performing today. (Courtesy of Mike Stosich.)

Harry James plays his trumpet at the Willowbrook Ballroom in May 1972. He was one of America's most highly acclaimed trumpet players and big band leaders during the swing era. He played with Benny Goodman in the 1930s and was known for numerous recordings throughout the 1940s. One of his greatest hits was "You Made Me Love You (I Didn't Want to Do it)." He also appeared in the films *Syncopation*, *Private Buckaroo*, and *Springtime in the Rockies*. One well-publicized marriage was to actress Betty Grable, who posed for the pinup poster that World War II veterans crooned over. (Courtesy of Mike Stosich.)

Here is another photograph of the wildly popular Harry James in 1972. One of his most famous associations was with Frank Sinatra. James hired him for $75 a week at the inception of his world renowned musical career years earlier. It was Sinatra who gave the eulogy at James's funeral in 1983. (Courtesy of Mike Stosich.)

Harry James plays another song in full swing, with his orchestra and drummer Les DeMerle in the back. (Courtesy of Mike Stosich.)

This photograph of the Harry James Orchestra at the Willowbrook Ballroom in 1972 shows drum virtuoso Les DeMerle performing with the band. James referred to him as "the best all-around drummer he ever had." The popular musician has toured with Wayne Newton and the Manhattan Transfer, as well as making appearances with Tony Bennett, Lou Rawls, and Frank Sinatra. The dynamic DeMerle also performed on Harry James's 1982 Grammy Award–winning album and later became an orchestra leader himself. (Courtesy of Mike Stosich.)

This is another of photograph of Harry James and His Orchestra playing at the Willowbrook in November 1978. They performed frequently at the Willowbrook, as well as other ballrooms and venues around the country for decades. (Courtesy of Mike Stosich.)

This signed promotional photograph of Harry James playing his trumpet hangs on the walls of the Willowbrook Ballroom's office, along with dozens of other pictures of performers, in memory of the days when he dazzled thousands of enchanted fans. This photograph was taken around the 1980s. (Courtesy of Birute Jodwalis.)

This 1978 photograph features the smiling faces of generous photograph contributor Mike Stosich, wife Elizabeth, and friend Marilyn Szostak sitting on a bench outside of the Willowbrook Ballroom during the intermission of a Glenn Miller Orchestra performance, as advertised on the marquee above them. (Courtesy of Mike Stosich.)

This photograph from the same night in 1978 shows the Glenn Miller Orchestra bus. As noted on the bus, Jimmy Henderson directed the band at that time. There were several Glenn Miller ghost bands that formed after Miller's disappearance during World War II. While on a trip to entertain US troops stationed in France, Miller's plane encountered inclement weather, and the plane went down. Tragically, Miller's body was never recovered. The celebrated performer was just 40 years old when it was broadcast that he had disappeared over the English Channel. He was a celebrated trombonist, composer, and orchestra leader. A few of his signature pieces include "In the Mood," "Moonlight Serenade," and "Chattanooga Choo Choo." (Courtesy of Mike Stosich.)

Jimmy Henderson plays his trombone during the same performance in 1978, as he once again leads the Glenn Miller Orchestra. (Courtesy of Mike Stosich.)

Here is a photograph of Jimmy Henderson (far right) with unidentified vocalists during the days when he led the Glenn Miller Orchestra and performed at the Willowbrook in 1978. Henderson was a multitalented musician who started piano lessons at age six, trombone lessons at age eight, and joined the Musicians Association at age 13. Henderson freelanced as a trombonist for more than 20 years before fronting the Glenn Miller Orchestra from 1975 until 1981, engaging audiences at a variety of events and venues. (Courtesy of Mike Stosich.)

A young, unidentified female vocalist performs with Jimmy Henderson and the Glenn Miller Orchestra in 1978. (Courtesy of Mike Stosich.)

A young, unidentified male vocalist performs with Jimmy Henderson and the Glenn Miller Orchestra in 1978. Even with the disco craze of the 1970s, masses of people still enjoyed live orchestra performances and dancing at ballrooms, much like today. (Courtesy of Mike Stosich.)

This advertisement promotes Don Glaser, a saxophone and clarinet player and talented arranger. His satiny sound was referred to as music as smooth as silk. His amazing musical career spanned five decades, with frequent performances in the Midwest, including the Willowbrook and various hotels and ballrooms. His dedicated wife of 40 years, Lois Costello, sang vocals and kept the band going despite Glaser suffering a series of strokes that left him partially paralyzed. (Courtesy of Mike Stosich.)

WILLOWBROOK
WHERE THE BIG BANDS PLAY
DINE, DANCE, ROMANCE
$7⁹⁵
NOW APPEARING
DON GLASSER ORCHESTRA
DINERS DANCE FREE

839-1000
581-1676

8900 ARCHER
WILLOW SPRING

Displayed here is an older advertisement for big band entertainment (a type of music rooted in jazz) at Willowbrook. It was most popular in the early 1930s through the late 1950s but continues on today. A big band typically consists of one or two dozen musicians and contains saxophones, trumpets, trombones, a rhythm section, and a vocalist. (Courtesy of Mike Stosich.)

This is a photograph of the outside of Willowbrook Ballroom as it appears while driving east down Archer Avenue. The alluring ballroom, with English Tudor-style architecture, boasts plenty of free parking and continues to draw thousands of dancers, entertainers, and partygoers who also attend private functions in the banquet rooms that stream from every direction of the dance floor. Executive chef Enrique Garcia has been a huge part of the success of the Willowbrook dining and banquet experience. In his 30 years of service, he has custom-created special menus suited to the style of the occasion. (Courtesy of Birute Jodwalis.)

The advertisement here is from the 1960s and features Harry James and his orchestra with former actress Joanie O'Brien as vocalist. O'Brien costarred with Cary Grant, Elvis, and John Wayne. Also featured is Ernie Andrews, a vocalist who was with James for six years. Sonny Payne is advertised as the drummer. (Courtesy of Mike Stosich.)

Les Brown is shown here in 1971 with singer Butch Stone. The song "A Good Man is Hard to Find" is one of their many music collaborations. The amazingly successful Les Brown Orchestra also functioned as a house band for top-notch talents, such as Steve Allen and Dean Martin. Brown also associated with Frank Sinatra and Ella Fitzgerald. Superstar Tony Bennett made his first public appearance with Les and his band. (Courtesy of Mike Stosich.)

Butch Stone sings vocals with Les Brown and his orchestra. Doris Day and many other singers joined with Brown during his performances. Brown was a big band leader and composer for almost seven decades and was frequently referred to as "Les Brown and his Band of Renown." Les and his band were noted for performing with Bob Hope on television, radio, and stage for nearly five decades. (Courtesy of Mike Stosich.)

A young man sits on the side of the stage during a Les Brown performance in 1971. John Verderbar refused to sell liquor at the venue for about three decades and encouraged families to bring their kids to the ballroom to enjoy the dancing and entertainment. (Courtesy of Mike Stosich.)

After Les Brown's demise in 2001, his son Les Brown Jr.—an actor, rock musician, producer, and concert promoter—took over his father's band. (Courtesy of Mike Stosich.)

To Pat — who runs the best ballroom in the mid-west! Always a pleasure! Les Brown

LES BROWN   THE BAND OF RENOWN

This promotional signed photograph of Les Brown is on display in the Willowbrook office. In addition to his autograph, his note refers to the Willowbrook as the "best ballroom in the Midwest." (Courtesy of Birute Jodwalis.)

From left to right, Helen Carig Verderbar, Les Brown, and Pat Verderbar Williams take the time to pose for a friendly photograph around the 1980s. (Courtesy of Birute Jodwalis.)

Freddy Martin and his orchestra are playing the Willowbrook in this 1967 photograph. An accomplished tenor saxophonist and bandleader, he was a pioneer of the tenor band style and fronted an all-tenor saxophone section. Nicknamed Mr. Silvertone, he was idolized and admired by many other saxophonists, jazz musicians, and fans—not just for his talent but because he was known as an incredibly nice guy. Martin led his pal Guy Lombardo's band for a few years during Lombardo's illness. (Courtesy of Mike Stosich.)

Guy Lombardo, shown here, started as a Canadian, later becoming an American, bandleader and violinist who graced the stage at the Willowbrook in 1971. The passionate musician formed his first orchestra with his brother while still in grammar school, practicing in the back of their father's tailor shop. Lombardo played for 30 years in New York City, and the band's famous broadcasts at the Waldorf Astoria were a huge part of New Year's Eve broadcasts across the nation. Even after his death, the holiday special continued on CBS for two more years. Noted for "Auld Lang Syne," their renowned recording of the token song still opens the festivities in Times Square on New Year's Eve. (Used with permission of Charles C. Sengstock.)

Guy Lombardo is shown here with part of his orchestra. He packed in the crowds when he played at the Willowbrook and any other venue. Lombardo's gregarious personality and good humor lent him an amiable rapport with the audience. He was also a champion speedboat racer who won many titles in the 1940s and 1950s and once set a world record. (Used with permission of Charles C. Sengstock.)

Bob Crosby, Bing Crosby's brother, performs at the Willowbrook in 1969. Some of the band members included Yank Lawson (trumpet), Gil Rodin (tenor and saxophone), Matty Matlock (clarinet), Bob Haggart (bass), and Billy Butterfield (trumpet). (Courtesy of Mike Stosich.)

Crosby is shown here with his orchestra in 1969. Arrangements for the orchestra were frequently the result of the talent of young trumpeter Gilbert Portmore, a decorated fighter pilot in the South Pacific during World War II. Although Crosby fronted the band— pleasing audiences with his charisma, good looks, and humor regarding life with his famous family ties—the orchestra was actually led by saxophone player Gil Rodin. Although Bob Crosby's voice had a similar soothing sound to Bing's, it lacked the same range. The good-natured humorist was quoted as saying, "I'm the only guy in the business who made it without any talent." (Courtesy of Mike Stosich.)

This 1969 photograph of Bob Crosby's Orchestra features his son Chris singing vocals. (Courtesy of Mike Stosich.)

This similar photograph of the Bob Crosby Orchestra with Chris singing lead shows a crowd of dance enthusiasts filling the dance floor right up to the front of the stage. (Courtesy of Mike Stosich.)

This photograph shows Harry James playing at the Willowbrook in 1970. The Harry James Orchestra was once considered the leading band in the United States. Photograph contributor Mike Stosich recalls driving by the Willowbrook in the 1970s and seeing James' name on the marquee, noting that back then it was only $4.50 to be entertained by this phenomenal orchestra leader and musician, less than it cost to go to a drive-in movie. Record-breaking crowds attended his every performance. (Courtesy of Mike Stosich.)

Harry James jams again with his orchestra in the same 1970 performance. (Courtesy of Mike Stosich.)

This is another shot of famous orchestra leader Harry James playing with his band in 1970. (Courtesy of Mike Stosich.)

Harry James continues performing and dazzling the audience. In 1942, James was billed as the top band of the whole country, and 30 years later, he was still going strong. (Courtesy of Mike Stosich.)

The young man in this 1970 photograph is Jack Watson playing the saxophone with the Harry James Orchestra. (Courtesy of Mike Stosich.)

The Harry James Orchestra is shown here, featuring an unidentified clarinet player. (Courtesy of Mike Stosich.)

As James and the orchestra continue playing in this 1970 photograph, both children and adults gather around the stage for a closer look at the performers. (Courtesy of Mike Stosich.)

This 1970 photograph features talented tenor saxophone player Corky Corcoran, who performed both solo and with the Harry James Orchestra for many years. In 1943, he appeared with Harry James and Lucille Ball in a musical comedy called *Best Foot Forward*. In his later years, he became known for playing a Leblanc 120Bb Paris saxophone with a silver-plated body and bow. This model became the company's signature saxophone and was named the Corky Corcoran Model. Today, the tenor saxophone 120 is gaining more recognition and respect as a result. (Courtesy of Mike Stosich.)

This 1970 photograph of the Harry James Orchestra features Sonny Payne as the drummer. Payne played with Count Basie for more than 10 years. In 1966, he joined up with Harry James and was also a staff drummer for Sinatra. Payne was a showman noted for throwing his drumsticks high into the air, almost to the ceiling, and catching them without fail, a feat that impressed audiences everywhere. (Courtesy of Mike Stosich.)

Young vocalist Glenn Rey was one of a parade of vocalists who sang with Harry James and his orchestra. This photograph was taken in 1970 at the ballroom. (Courtesy of Mike Stosich.)

Glenn Rey is featured again, tickling the ivories at the same 1970 performance. (Courtesy of Mike Stosich.)

Harry James is standing behind vocalist Cathy Kimmy, shown here in 1970. The singer was one in a huge lineup of many performers who shared the spotlight with Harry James and his orchestra during his active, lifelong music career. (Courtesy of Mike Stosich.)

This is a band that Dick Jurgens assembled in the late 1960s. He toured with them until the mid-1970s. Although no one in the photograph is identified with certainty, it is know that Buddy Moreno and Harry Cool were performers and that, on the night of this performance, Ray McInstry performed an alto solo. Jurgens, a swing music bandleader and trumpeter, was initially very active in the 1930s and 1940s, with singer Eddy Howard playing a significant role in the band's long journey of success. One of Jurgen's biggest hits was "One Dozen Roses." (Courtesy of Mike Stosich.)

Enjoy Dining

willow-brook

in the colorful surroundings of the

Willow-Brook Room
DANCING EVERY WED.,
THURS., FRI., SAT. & SUN.

SUNDAY DINNER 12 NOON
AFTERNOON TEA DANCING
2:30 P.M. to 6 P.M.

"Bring a Friend or Meet a Friend"

OPENING
WED. AUG. 16
DICK JURGENS
& HIS ORCH.
"HERE'S THAT BAND AGAIN"

the willow-brook

BALLROOM-RESTAURANT
8900 South Archer Rd., Willow Springs, Ill.
Phone TE 9-1000 and LU 1-1676

This 1970 advertisement promoting Dick Jurgens with "Here's that Band Again" testifies to his popularity and frequent appearances at the Willowbrook and other venues. Note the differing phone number and days of operation. (Courtesy of Mike Stosich.)

This unknown orchestra is thought to possibly be an in-house band called the Willowbrook Orchestra, however, its identity is not certain. (Courtesy of Birute Jodwalis.)

This newspaper photograph shows the enticing 6,000-square-foot maple sprung dance floor when Willowbrook was called the Oh Henry Ballroom. Literally millions of dancers glided across the floor while countless orchestras entertained on stage. (Courtesy of Mike Stosich.)

This 1981 newspaper shows an old photograph of John Verderbar (seated) and his sons Ed (left) and Rudy. The father-and-sons team owned and operated the Oh Henry Ballroom–turned–Willowbrook Ballroom for decades. At the time this photograph was printed, the Verderbar men were deceased, and the ballroom was under the helm of Ed's wife, Helen, and daughter Pat Williams Verderbar. (Courtesy of Mike Stosich.)

Shown in this 1981 photograph is Pat Williams Verderbar (left), who then functioned as the owner and manager of the Willowbrook Ballroom and restaurant. Her mother, Helen Carig Verderbar, is seated on the right. The establishment is readying to celebrate 60 years in business with a rare public appearance by Peter Duchin and his orchestra. (Courtesy of Mike Stosich.)

This old photograph of the Oh Henry Room from the *Southtown Economist* newspaper shows a picture of the ballroom, however, the date of the fire was in June 1930, not 1925, as noted on the picture. Numerous other articles, family members, and historians attest to the date of the disaster. (Courtesy of Mike Stosich.)

This is another photograph of orchestra leader Pete Duchin, who played at the Willowbrook's 60th anniversary celebration in 1981. (Courtesy of Mike Stosich.)

This photograph of Myron Floren, who played accordion since the age of six, was taken in 2004 when he played at the Willowbrook Ballroom. Floren was the accordionist on the *Lawrence Welk Show* from 1950 to 1982. His trademark song was "Lady of Spain." He was inducted into the International Polka Music Hall of Fame in 1990. In 1996, the American Accordionists Association honored his achievements. (Courtesy of Birute Jodwalis.)

This photograph of the Lawrence Welk Orchestra was taken during a performance at the Willowbrook in 1971. Dick Dale sang "One Cup of Happiness" with the entire Welk Orchestra. Vocalists Sandi Griffiths and Sally Flynn sang "I'm Gonna Sit Right Down and Write Myself a Letter," and "I Got Love." The band also appeared there in the 1960s. This is the same photograph used for the cover but a larger version showing more of the band members. (Courtesy of Mike Stosich.)

A jam-packed dance floor of people celebrated the Willowbrook's 75th anniversary in 1996 while the Tommy Dorsey ghost band played at the event. The Christmas and New Year's holidays are often the busiest time of year for the business, with both private and company parties. (Courtesy of Birute Jodwalis.)

The Tommy Dorsey Orchestra, shown here under the leadership of Buddy Morrow, performs at the Willowbrook's 75th anniversary celebration where the ballroom, in conjunction with the United States Postal Service, launched a commemorative stamp series on September 12, 1996. It honored big band legends, such as Count Basie, Tommy and Jimmy Dorsey, Benny Goodman, and Glenn Miller, all of whom played at the Willowbrook at some point. The gala featured additional entertainment by Nan Mason and Johnny Gabor. The lobby of the ballroom was turned temporarily into an official postal station, offering its own Willowbrook postmark. (Courtesy of Birute Jodwalis.)

CAROL MOSELEY-BRAUN
ILLINOIS

United States Senate

WASHINGTON, D. C. 20510-1303

February 15, 1996

Mr. and Mrs. Richard Williams
Willowbrook Ballroom and
  Banquet Center
8900 S. Archer Road
Willow Springs, Illinois 60480

Dear Mr. and Mrs. Williams:

I would like to congratulate the Chicagoland Willowbrook Ballroom on its 75th Anniversary.

For seventy-five years the Chicagoland Willowbrook Ballroom has enthralled Chicagoans with its elegance. You have no doubt left an indellible mark in the history of the city, which has helped to create special moments for literally thousands of people.
On this wonderful occasion, I extend my warmest wishes for many more years of success and service. I and all of Chicago thank you.

Once again, congratulations on your seventy-five years!

Yours truly,

Carol Moseley-Braun
United States Senator

CMB : qw

US Senator Carol Mosley-Braun, along with other politicians and dignitaries, sent congratulatory letters to Willowbrook owners Dick and Pat Williams in honor of their big 75-year anniversary bash in 1996. (Courtesy of Birute Jodwalis.)

Sally Roberts is shown here in 1991, when she played with the Bill Kokos Orchestra, which was known for its big band sounds in the 1940s and 1950s. The band, known for its sweet sophisticated swing, continually kept big band music alive at the Willowbrook and other ballrooms because, as Roberts put it, "even young people like dancing cheek to cheek." Formerly a country singer, Roberts had no problem making the transition to this genre of music. (Courtesy of Birute Jodwalis.)

In addition to being an orchestra leader, Bill Kokos played the alto saxophone, clarinet, and drums. This 1990s article from *Dancing USA* has a short biography on Kokos, revealing that his claim to fame came when his band played at a special reunion for Pres. Harry S. Truman, with a host of celebrities in attendance, including Ronald Reagan. Kokos had a sign in his successful insurance business that read, "Life without music would be a mistake." He also stated in an interview that it was serendipity that led him to find Roberts to sing with his band. (Courtesy of Birute Jodwalis.)

Dancing USA
ROMANCE OF BALLROOM DANCE

BIG BAND REPORT
"Yesterday and Today" By Jack Lebo

Coo-coo over Kokos

Bill Kokos, of Calumet City, Ill., is not only a successful insurance agent, but also a highly respected orchestra leader. As you walk into his office, a huge sign on the wall grabs your attention — "LIFE WITH-OUT MUSIC WOULD BE A MISTAKE."

Bill began his musical training in high school, playing alto sax, clarinet and drums. He was a member of the Woodlawn Area Chicago Boys Club Band and played for weekly dances. He called his outfit, "Bill Kokos & His Musical Tops" and used the slogan, "Spin Along With Bill." Following his graduation in 1949, Bill played with several bands, and with the threat of the draft facing him, auditioned for the 5th Armored Division Band at Ft. Sheridan, Ill.

One of his fondest memories was playing for President Harry S. Truman in his hometown. Added Bill, "It was some sort of reunion and many celebrities were there, including then-actor Ronald Reagan."

Following his Army stint, this maestro became active in the American Legion and joined a band. Eventually, Bill and a group of other musicians formed their own dance band. They purchased some fine arrangements by Jurgens, Lombardo, Miller, Howard, Garber, Kaye and a host of others. After a year and a half of perfecting their sound, the orchestra was prepared to let the world hear their music.

According to Kokos, "Things really started happening when we hired vocalist Sally Roberts. We are now well established and in demand by the dancing and listening public."

The band has "hit the road" in 1994. They opened "The Most Beautiful Ballroom In The World," the prestigeous Indiana Roof in Indianapolis, having been selected from over 30 competing bands. As one big band fan was overheard to say, "Folks are going coo-coo over Kokos!" Contact: 592 Torrence Ave., Calumet City, IL, (708) 891-8582.

BILL KOKOS - He'll insure you that the music's great.

Tommy Sands was a teen idol, singer, and actor in the 1950s. He performed at the Willowbrook Ballroom in 1992 for an ultimate 1950s rock 'n' roll dance party. Sands starting playing guitar at eight years old, and by the age of nine, he was working part-time at a radio station. His first record deal came at age 15. His song "Teenage Crush" reached No. 3 on the Billboard Hot 100 Chart. (Courtesy of Birute Jodwalis.)

TOMMY SANDS

An advertisement for Tommy Sands's upcoming Willowbrook performance is shown here. Proceeds for the event were donated to the National Music Foundation. In addition to his recording contract, Sands starred in several movies, including *Mardi Gras*, *Babes in Toyland* (with female teen idol Annette Funicello), and *The Longest Day* with John Wayne and Henry Fonda. Sands married Nancy Sinatra, daughter of singing sensation and actor Frank Sinatra, in the 1960s. (Courtesy of Birute Jodwalis.)

Although the identification of this band is not certain, the autograph of Tom Traynor is clear. The current owners of the Willowbrook believe this group may be one of the many swing bands that performed before they took ownership in 1997. (Courtesy of Birute Jodwalis.)

This is another unknown band that played at the Willowbrook Ballroom around the 1980s. It may have been part of the 1960s rock bands that performed for the Friday night lineup in the 1980s, but identification is uncertain. (Courtesy of Birute Jodwalis.)

Six

THE WILLOWBROOK BALLROOM TODAY

The Ron Smolen Orchestra performed at the Willowbrook in 1990. The 10-piece orchestra showcases the sounds of drums, a piano, vocals, bass, four saxophones, two trumpets, and one trombone. Smolen started playing the accordion at age six and later learned the clarinet and saxophone. The Ron Smolen Orchestra has played at events across the United States, including dinner dances, lavish weddings, festivals, theaters, casinos, and ballrooms. They have also been heard on radio stations. (Courtesy of Birute Jodwalis.)

JOHN MUELLER as BUDDY HOLLY

This promotional shot of John Mueller, who performs every January at the ballroom, is on display on the office walls of the Willowbrook. The tribute band includes John Mueller as Buddy Holly, Big Bopper Jr. as Big Bopper Sr., and, originally, Fernando Vega played the role of Ritchie Valens. Holly was best remembered for being a pioneer of rock 'n' roll with megahits, such as "That'll Be the Day," "Everyday," "True Love Ways," "Maybe Baby," and "Peggy Sue." (Courtesy of Birute Jodwalis.)

This is a promotional shot of J.P. Richardson, also known as Big Bopper Jr., who honors the memory of his father by imitating him onstage. Each member, whether related or not, bears a striking resemblance to the entertainer they imitate. Big Bopper's signature song was "Chantilly Lace." (Courtesy of Birute Jodwalis.)

Nephew Fernando Vega originally played the part of his uncle Ritchie Valens for a short time, as shown here in this promotional photograph. (Courtesy of Birute Jodwalis.)

FERNANDO VEGA AS RITCHIE VALENS

Ray Anthony (left) took over playing the role of Ritchie Valens in the tribute band of this Willowbrook photograph from January 2008. Valens, a pioneer of Spanish-speaking rock 'n' roll, found the road to fame with songs like "LaBamba," "Donna," and "Let's Go." (Courtesy of Birute Jodwalis.)

Liz Harris and Lou Holly stand at the Willowbrook stage where the Winter Dance Party Tour will be playing once again. They cover events for their 1950s to 1960s nostalgia magazine, *Keep Rockin'*. (Courtesy of Liz Harris.)

Winter Dance Party Tour

AS SEEN ON THE JERRY LEWIS TELETHON & VH-1

John Mueller as

BIG BOPPER
"CHANTILLY LACE"

J. P. RICHARDSON JR.

BUDDY HOLLY

RITCHIE VALENS
"DONNA"
"COME ON LETS GO"

Ray Anthony

Special Guest

WILLOWBROOK BALLROOM!
Willow Springs, IL   JAN 19th
Call 708-839-1000 For Ticket info

"John Mueller is living proof that Buddy Holly's legacy will live on." -Chicago Tribune

FOR MORE INFORMATION VISIT WWW.YOURBUDDYJOHN.COM

This is a signed flyer of the Holly, Bopper, and Valens tribute band. The Winter Dance Party Tour has been a sellout for the past 10 years, receiving rave reviews from fans who return regularly for the yearly performance. (Courtesy of Don McKenna.)

Big Bopper Jr. (left) takes a moment to pose with Liz Harris and Lou Holly at the Willowbrook Ballroom during the tribute band's show on January 16, 2009. (Courtesy of Liz Harris.)

Here the crowd supports and applauds the tribute band by moving closer to the stage. The original trio of entertainers—including Buddy Holly, the Big Bopper, and Ritchie Valens—lost their lives in a plane crash, along with their pilot, but their music lives on through this tribute band. Don McLean refers to that tragic day in 1959 as the day the music died in his song "American Pie." (Courtesy of Liz Harris.)

Lou Holly, co-owner and editor, is shown here with fiancée Liz Harris, co-owner and publisher of *Keep Rockin'* magazine. They promoted their first issue at the Willowbrook Ballroom. Note the cover showing Big Bopper from a previous performance. (Courtesy of Liz Harris.)

Liz Harris and Lou Holly display a February 2009 issue of *Keep Rockin'* magazine at the entrance of the ballroom. The cover of the February issue depicts a feature story on the Big Bopper. February is the month of the tragic accident that took the lives of Big Bopper, Buddy Holly, and Ritchie Valens. (Courtesy of Liz Harris.)

The three little ponytailed girls shown here are Heidi, Ava, and Olivia. They are dressed up in poodle skirts and 1950s garb as they enjoy dancing during the tribute band's intermission in January 2008. (Courtesy of Liz Harris.)

The late Betty McKenna and her granddaughter Ava Barchak stop to pose during intermission. Betty was an employee at the Willowbrook for 28 years, functioning in various capacities, from hosting to selling tickets, checking coats, and setting tables. Husband Don McKenna, a director of the Willow Springs Historical Society, also worked at the Willowbrook Ballroom, where he parked cars for a brief period as a teenager in the 1950s. (Courtesy of Don McKenna.)

Enthusiastic fans move to the front of the stage to get a closer look as the entertainers of the tribute band delight the audience with some of the early days of rock 'n' roll. (Courtesy of Liz Harris.)

This is a close-up shot of Big Bopper Jr. performing on the Willowbrook stage during the tribute performance. In addition to imitating his father's songs, he is also noted for his nostalgic humor. (Courtesy of Liz Harris.)

Current Willowbrook owners Gedas (left) and Birute Jodwalis (right) pose with entertainer Jorge Santana during a Valentine's Day performance in 2008. Jorge's band, Malo, is known for hit songs "Suavecito" and "Nena." (Courtesy of Birute Jodwalis.)

Jorge Santana is seated third from left, posing with the entire Malo band. Also shown in this 2009 photograph are Gedas Jodwalis, standing second from the left, and Birute Jodwalis, standing fourth from left. Other members are unidentified. Malo earned four gold records. Their first album soared to the top of the charts at No. 2. Jorge toured with his brother Carlos after a long split. (Courtesy of Birute Jodwalis.)

Beatles tribute band American English started playing at the Willowbrook Ballroom in 2008 and became a quick favorite. This is their promotional photograph. The band members are, from left to right, Eric Michaels as Paul, Doug Couture as George, Tom Gable as Ringo, and Young Hines as John. Hines left the group in 2010. (Courtesy of Glenn Jones.)

Here, the Beatles tribute band performs the Abbey Road segment of their act, which features monster hits like "Something" and "Come Together," at the Willowbrook Ballroom. (Courtesy of Glenn Jones.)

116

Enthusiastic dancers cannot seem to get enough of phenomenally popular tribute band American English. The band has a huge following at local fests, venues, and sold-out theaters. The band played in Liverpool at original Beatles venues, including Cavern Beat, and has received major media attention. The group also appeared on *190 North* with Paul McCartney. (Courtesy of Glenn Jones.)

This photograph features American English performing Beatles hits from the early years of their inception, which includes songs like "Help," "A Hard Day's Night," and "I Saw Her Standing There." Fans and dancers approach the stage for a closer look. Costumes are authentic and changed for each segment, according to the time period and music. (Courtesy of Glenn Jones.)

This is another shot of American English performing the early Beatle songs that make for a happy trip down memory lane. Some prefer to watch the band and sing along, while others like to kick up their heels to their favorite songs, as shown at this 2008 performance. (Courtesy of Glenn Jones.)

American English performs; this time the crowd is entertained by the Sergeant Pepper set, and the band has changed costumes. "A Day in the Life" and "Lucy in the Sky with Diamonds" are just a couple of the nostalgic songs that keep audiences coming back for more. (Courtesy of Glenn Jones.)

The Good Time Charley Singles Dance Club unites with singles from the Plenty of Fish online dating website for a huge dance party in January 2011. Shown here are line dancers doing the "Cupid Shuffle." DJ Fast Freddy spins the tunes as participants enjoy a wide variety of music and dances, such as salsa, disco, jitterbug, Latin, and line and slow dancing. (Courtesy of Steven Fluke.)

Ziggy Bejger Jr. and longtime sweetheart Donna Jaklich enjoy some fancy moves at the combined Good Time Charley and Plenty of Fish singles dance party. Both have been coming to the Willowbrook for many years, enjoying the dancing and socialization, as well as the enticing dance floor and variety of music. Ziggy remembers his parents taking him to the ballroom for various special events since the age of four. Like so many others, he has been a fan of the venue his entire life. (Courtesy of Steven Fluke.)

Ziggy Bejger Jr. and Donna Jaklich stop for a photograph between dance steps. These combined singles dances attract hundreds of dancers and spectators who come back again and again to enjoy the huge dance floor. (Courtesy of Steven Fluke.)

Dennis Bowling of the Good Time Charley singles group and Dara Bottenhagen with the Plenty of Fish singles take a break at the Carousel Bar after several spins on the dance floor at the January 2011 event. (Courtesy of Steven Fluke.)

Mike and Bonnie (last names unknown) share a hug and a break from kicking up their heels on their favorite dance floor. (Courtesy of Steven Fluke.)

Shown here are unidentified dancers from the combined singles dance at the Willowbrook Ballroom. A frequent event usually occurring every other Friday night from 8 p.m. until midnight, it brings in hundreds of dancers from the Chicagoland and Midwest area. These dances have become so popular that some have traveled hundreds of miles to attend, sometimes making a weekend trip out of it. (Courtesy of Steven Fluke.)

Karen Frost and Alex Orfanos from the Plenty of Fish singles group are friends who love to dance and socialize with the crowds. Alex has been taking salsa, tango, swing, and rumba lessons at the ballroom for several weeks. He also enjoys an occasional visit to the Sunday ballroom dances where big band orchestras like the Teddy Lee Orchestra, Steve Cooper, and Steve Anthony continue to dazzle the audience. (Courtesy of Steven Fluke.)

Happy couple Joy Vastola and Marty Walker seem to be having a great time at the Willowbrook Ballroom as they dance to both the romantic slow songs and the rock 'n' roll tunes. This was Marty's first time at the Willowbrook, but most newcomers return because they are drawn to the huge dance floor, the music, and the ambiance of this historical venue. (Courtesy of Steven Fluke.)

Gayle Anson and Alex Orfanos became friends through the Plenty of Fish singles group and enjoy kicking up their heels on the immense dance floor that draws hundreds of singles once or twice a month. (Courtesy of Steven Fluke.)

Karen Frost and Steve Sanford are also friends who met through the Plenty of Fish singles dances. They are shown here at a combined singles dance in January 2011. Both love to dance and mingle with the crowd from beginning until end. (Courtesy of Steven Fluke.)

This is a photograph of the 6,000-square-foot maple sprung dance floor that literally millions of dancers have glided across or stomped upon over the past nine decades, doing everything from the jitterbug and the twist to the salsa and the swing. In 2000, the Willowbrook was profiled as one of America's "glorious, historic, legendary, treasured ballroom dance floors" by *Amateur Dancer* magazine. There have also been documentaries about the ballroom and its colorful history on PBS. (Courtesy of Steven Fluke.)

Shown here in January 2011 is Charley Shanks, standing in the lobby with photographs of the Willowbrook's many banquet rooms displayed on the wall behind him. The Good Time Charley Singles Dances currently run every other Friday at the ballroom, drawing hundreds of dancers. He has held dances there intermittently for almost two decades. (Courtesy of Steven Fluke.)

Shown here again in January 2011 is Charley Shanks, the originator of the Good Time Charley Singles Dances, the longest running singles dances in the Chicagoland area. Shanks started the dances in 1990 to provide a meeting place for singles to dance and mingle. Interestingly, he met his wife, Mary, at one of his Willowbrook dances in 1991. (Courtesy of Steven Fluke.)

This is a January 2011 photograph of the Carousel Bar with its carnival-like lighting, a favorite place for people to have a drink, linger, and watch the dance floor when they need a break or desire a quiet place to talk and relax between dances. (Courtesy of Steven Fluke.)

This is a photograph of Joe Waickus working behind the popular Carousel Bar. He has been employed at the Willowbrook for over a decade. Nolan Robinson, another long-term employee, has been a bartender here for over 25 years. (Courtesy of Birute Jodwalis.)

Shown here is the larger, more conspicuous, wrought-iron spider and web that architect William Sevic designed and displayed after he constructed the ballroom. It is currently covered with fabric behind the stage. (Courtesy of Steven Fluke.)

www.arcadiapublishing.com

MAP SEARCH

Discover books about the town where you grew up, the cities where your friends and families live, the town where your parents met, or even that retirement spot you've been dreaming about. Our Web site provides history lovers with exclusive deals, advanced notification about new titles, e-mail alerts of author events, and much more.

Find Your Place in History.